SHARING A VISION

The History of the Orinda Country Club ORINDA, CALIFORNIA

BARBARA FULLER

6

Contents

DEDICATION

To the deLaveaga family, and to the countless friends, staff, employees, and former members whose lives have inspired this Club history

PRESIDENT'S LETTER

The deLaveaga family had the foresight and courage to develop the Country Club and the surrounding community that we know and enjoy as Orinda. Orinda Country Club was much more than just a golf course to so many who have passed before us. It was a weekend respite from "overcrowded" cities, a relaxing country retreat from the daily toil, and a place to enjoy camaraderie and the hospitality of friends and family; to swim and picnic and play that new game called golf; to join in a few sets of tennis, enjoy dinner, and even stay overnight.

While some things have changed since the inception, the gracious traditions of our Club family have endured, grown, and prospered. Through the efforts and foresight of those in the past and with your continuing dedication in the present, Orinda Country Club will long endure.

For many years there have been plans to document and record the history of the Orinda Country Club. Without the devotion and endless hours of research, interviews, and record keeping by Del Loper, who chairs our History Committee, this volume would never have come to life. Assisting her were committee members Frank Brunk, Jr., Joan Calder, Earl Cunha, Ruth and Wally Riddell, and Kathleen Woolsey. On behalf of the membership I thank them for recording our history to be relived and enjoyed by present and future members for many years to come.

Doug Gillespie
President—1991

FOREWORD

In your hands today are the memories of yesterday, chronicled for posterity in the form of history.

At the time of Orinda Country Club's fiftieth anniversary celebration in 1974, the source of information used for our early history was a frequent column in *Orindans* written by past president Jeff Hedemark, "Remember When." Along with these columns, the Anniversary Committee began collecting old *Orindans*, interviewing founding members, and searching for trophies and memorabilia, scrapbooks, and old newspaper clippings. Later, at an "old-timers dinner," an oral history was presented. From then on Club trivia and accomplishments continued to be collected and displayed, and they formed for us a vivid tapestry of the past. The Board of Directors in 1988 determined that we should produce a book for the membership to serve as a vehicle to help each of us understand the past and assist us in having a greater respect for current Club life.

The fact that many second- and third-generation families are continuing the traditions of OCC is proof that the diverse activities

available for various ages continue to provide pleasure and friendships. Some members will remember specific events, times, and people; to them this chronicle may seem too limited.

But recognizing our desire for brevity, the History Book Committee is pleased to present this selection of items from the past to enhance your enjoyment of the future.

We thank the following people who supported our quest for accuracy and acknowledge the following sources:

Muir Sorrick—*The History of Orinda: Gateway to Contra Costa County* (Orinda Library Board, 1970); Robert Murdock—"Notes and Impressions" (Orinda Country Club history collection)

Ned deLaveaga, Joe Varney, Ray Dickey, Mike Hadden, Clarke Mathews, and Pat Patten—oral tapes; Mrs. John Bannister, Mrs. B. F. Brunk, Sr., Mr. and Mrs. Blake Calder, Mrs. Howard W. Crandall, Mr. and Mrs. Walter E. Cunha, Mr. and Mrs. Donald Doten, Mrs. William Jaekle, Mrs. Andrew McGlynn, Mr. and Mrs. Wallace Riddell, Mrs. G. Arthur Somers, Mrs. Jay Spongberg, and Mr. and Mrs. Edgar B. Stewart —pictures, scrapbooks, and newspaper clippings

Considerable time has been spent in gathering this information, and we hope you will enjoy the result, knowing that this is but a sampling of the continuing accomplishments of your Club.

The History Book Committee

THE MAKINGS OF A CLUB

The Concept

8

When Edward deLaveaga first conceived of the Orinda Country Club in the 1920s, he intended it to be a focal point for life in the newly developing community around it. At that time, few people lived on the beautiful wooded land in the hills east of Oakland across the Bay from San Francisco. In fact, the growth of Orinda has been closely linked to the growth of OCC.

The Club was the center of activity that encouraged people to make the difficult journey in the days before the Bay Area Rapid Transit (BART) and the Caldecott Tunnel—days when it might take hours to drive to Orinda along the Old Tunnel Road, or along the tortuous San Pablo Dam Road or Fish Ranch Road. Some people parked their automobiles at the Grizzly Peak stables and rode horseback into Orinda, leaving their animals to be groomed at Miss Graham's Riding Academy on Orinda Way while they enjoyed their stay at the Country Club.

For the most part, this region was inhabited in the early 1900s by deer, coyotes, wildcats, raccoons, skunks,

and even grizzlies. But one of the few people who lived here, Edward deLaveaga, imagined a community where others from the city could come to enjoy the country life he knew. Edward, known by his friends as E. I., had grown up on his father's land in what was then called Orinda Park. He had heard his father's dream of sharing his beloved land with others and set himself the task of carrying out that dream.

E. I. was a determined young man with high standards and with the ability to foresee potential problems and prevent them from occurring. He knew if people were to come here, they would need water, and it would need to be inexpensive. They would need a village to provide services. And they would need something to entice them—something like a country club.

Thus E. I. began to work. He arranged for the building of Lake Cascade to provide water. He contracted with Hamilton Murdock, one of the foremost Spanish Mediterranean architects of the day, to design the village and the homes of Haciendas del Orinda in the style of Southern California's San Clemente. And he set about establishing the Orinda Country Club—first its beautiful freeform swimming pool; then a clubhouse, a five-hole golf course, and its first tennis court near the pool, now overlooking the eighteenth fairway; and finally a full program of social activities and an eighteen-hole golf course that would host the Northern California Golf Association (NCGA) tournament in 1928. This was to be a family club, a place where men, women, and children could recreate and enjoy one another's company.

So it began—a small club of new area inhabitants open for $500 to anyone who purchased a lot in Orinda. And so it is today—a central part of life for many families in Orinda and neighboring areas, now so popular that potential members willing to pay a $42,500 transfer fee must often wait several years for a membership to become available.

Cows graze on the land east of San Pablo Road in what is now the sixteenth and seventeenth fairways. The Pacific Gas and Electric power lines and towers seen here in the 1920s have been a source of controversy through the years but have never been moved. ◄

The deLaveaga Family

Of the few families that came to Orinda in the late 1800s and remained, one of the most influential was the deLaveaga family, beginning with brothers Miguel and Jose. The brothers' father, Jose Vicente deLaveaga, had come in 1857 from Mexico to San Francisco, where he was a banker and the owner of a water company. He had befriended San Francisco Mayor Andrew Jackson Bryant, who owned a lovely and well-known home in Orinda; Bryant may have introduced the deLaveaga family to the area. Whatever the case, Miguel and Jose were attracted by the beauty of the land, by the Spanish history of the area, and by the country life where the sun shone all the time, despite Orinda's proximity to San Francisco's fog belt. In 1887, they paid $50,880 for 1,178 acres, including the land on which the Orinda Country Club now stands. They divided their land and began building.

Miguel's home, *Bien Venida* (meaning welcome), was completed in 1888 on a knoll off Miner Road near San Pablo Creek, not far from the Country Club's present ninth fairway. The home burned down in 1915 but was reconstructed that same year and remains today a historic landmark, currently occupied by E. I.'s son, Ned, and Ned's wife, Alysone. E. I. and his older brother and sister spent much of their time at Bien Venida. E. I. particularly loved the land, often riding in the hills, fishing, and hunting. At a family gathering in 1914, his father said, "The land is becoming too valuable to hold. Someday we are going to have to give it away and sell the climate." E. I., then thirty, took the prophecy to heart.

The next year Miguel died, and by 1920 E. I. was the only member of his family still in the area. Sister Julia spent her time in San Francisco, and brother Vincent had gone to run the family ranch near Hollister. It was a time of national prosperity, when many were able to indulge in luxurious living, and also a time when the Oakland-Berkeley area was expanding—the perfect time for establishing a first-class development in the Orinda hills. With his strong love of the land and his acute sense of business, E. I. set about the task.

E. I. took things one step at a time, always planning for the needs of Orinda's future residents. First there were roads to build and extensive water systems to create. Lake Orinda (currently the Orinda Park Pool on El Toyonal) was constructed, as was the small subdivision of Orinda Park Terrace around the pool. With the success of that area, E. I. began immediately to set plans for a new, even more ambitious, 418-acre subdivision, to be called Haciendas del Orinda, and for a village, Lake Cascade, and the Orinda Country Club. He purchased some additional acreage from the Antonio Marshall family, who had bought it from Miguel's brother, Jose, thus acquiring all the land—a total of 581 acres—necessary for his latest project.

Visitors to the Club when it first opened in 1925 could walk down a path from the clubhouse to this rose garden, planted and tended by E. I. deLaveaga. From here, they could see the beautiful waterfall spilling from Lake Cascade into the pool. ◄

Lake Cascade and the Swimming Pool

homes, and a new water company was formed, with each person who purchased a lot in Haciendas del Orinda receiving one share. Amazingly, the engineering was so sound that the dam did not require strengthening to meet new standards until 1965. The lake itself was so beautiful with its flowers and majestic oaks that tourists came to it from San Francisco, the Peninsula, and all around the East Bay by motor carriage or on horseback.

Below the lake, construction of the swimming pool began. When completed in 1924, the free-form pool, resembling a mountain pond, was the largest of its type in the Bay Area; it remains the largest in Contra Costa County today. Bringing water from Lake Cascade down to a small landscaped pool and then to the larger pool surrounded by rocks was a thirty-five-foot waterfall patterned after the Blue Hole of the Mokelumne River. E. I. had fished at the Blue Hole in Calaveras County with his friend Hamilton Murdock, and Murdock had painted a watercolor picture of it, thus inspiring the waterfall at Orinda. At one end of the pool, behind a bamboo barrier, was a knee-high area for the little ones; across from the pool were lawns and picnic tables, swings, and a sandbox. These things, E. I. believed, would bring people to the area.

By 1922, Lake Cascade was complete. To make it, the workers had dammed the 18.5-acre valley into which Cascade Creek emptied. The basin was to hold some 62.74 million gallons of water. The water was filtered for use in Orinda

E. I. deLaveaga's foresightedness led to the building of Lake Cascade, a source of water for the Club through many subsequent droughts. The clubhouse currently occupies the site on the right of this picture. ◀

Haciendas del Orinda and the Village

E. I. deLaveaga purchased these commercial buildings on the left of Orinda Way to house workers during the construction of the clubhouse and the golf course in the 1920s. Behind them is the site of the sixteenth and seventeenth fairways. To the right of the road, near the bridge, is the old fire station, currently an antique store. ▶

In the meantime, work had begun on the new housing development, Haciendas del Orinda, with streets given Spanish names and homes to sell for $5,000 to $50,000. It was time, E. I. knew, to start work on the village as well. He contracted with Jimmy L'Hommedieu, a popular engineer, surveyor, and realty-company owner from Oakland, and with Hamilton Murdock, the San Francisco–trained architect who had made his name by heading the construction of such structures as San Francisco's De Young Building on Market Street. L'Hommedieu would be responsible for marketing the place, Murdock for building it. According to E. I.'s plans, the village—consisting of a firehouse (now an antique shop), Miss Graham's Riding Academy, a garage, a nursery, a village store, and other stores—was constructed on what is now Orinda Way.

To help their salespeople bring prospects to the new area in 1924, E. I. and L'Hommedieu provided them with a handbook filled with beautiful pictures of the area and containing the following advice: "In the selling of this proposition FORGET ALL REAL ESTATE! To successfully sell Haciendas del Orinda the *general idea* must be sold to the prospect first. . . . Never mention lot until your prospect has come to the tract, has covered it entirely and is fully enthused with the general thought of a country home at

Haciendas del Orinda. . . . Remember that you are dealing with people to whom courtesy and good manners are most important."

As a marketing brochure explained, "Orinda, a valley of appealing natural beauty . . . offers a complete change of climate and of scenery. . . . The days are always sunny. The hills are clothed in evergreen oaks and their lovely contour completes a delightful picture. . . . Orinda . . . was conceived as a place for family recreation, wholesome, happy country family life. There is something for every member of the family to do— golf, swimming, horseback riding, tennis, dancing, hiking. Playground for little children too!"

The Clubhouse and the Golf Course

While salespeople in the 1920s may have mentioned golf first, and while the sport is today the major attraction for many Club members, E. I. originally had no intention of facilitating such a pastime at his Club. A hunter and a fisherman, he had always cherished the pristine countryside, and he did not want to alter the landscape or remove the trees to make room for fairways. Fishing derbies, nature walks, and equestrian trails were of more interest to him. "He never would take up golf," says his son, Ned. "I don't think he ever touched a golf club."

But E. I.'s friend Jimmy L'Hommedieu, who had played at Claremont and Diablo country clubs, convinced him that golf was the upcoming sport and that an eighteen-hole course would be essential to the success of any upscale community. According to character, E. I. determined to have the best course possible if he was going to have one at all. He hired Willie Watson, a Scotsman who was internationally renowned as a golf-course architect. Watson had come to the States in 1898 and had designed several courses in the Midwest and Southern California as well as the courses at the Olympic Club, the Diablo Country Club, and the Berkeley Country Club (now known as Mira Vista).

History might have been different had Willie Watson not been hard up for cash just then. He and E. I. clashed early on, and it seemed at first that neither would give in. E. I. had already begun planning his clubhouse on a prominent rocky bluff where Jim Marshall's barn had once stood near the site of Lake Cascade. This did not make sense to Watson, who insisted that the first nine holes of the golf course must end at the clubhouse, with the tenth tee nearby. He thought the clubhouse should be located in the spot now surrounded by the second, third, and twelfth fairways, with easy access from Miner Road.

"Nonsense," said E. I. "My clubhouse is going to be on this cliff, and I don't care where the ninth or the tenth holes are located." To him, it was more important that his guests be able to look out across the beautiful San Pablo Valley from the balcony of their clubhouse, and he was willing to find a new golf-course architect if necessary to achieve that. Eventually Watson did give in—but even today OCC golfers playing nine holes must skip from the third to the thirteenth in order to end at the eighteenth green and the clubhouse.

The Opening

The foundations of the clubhouse had already been constructed by the time E. I. deLaveaga signed over a deed of conveyance to the directors of the Orinda Country Club on June 17, 1924. The transference of land consisted of about $450,000 in real property present and future, a total of about 159 acres, for which E. I. was to be paid over a period of many years. The costs of building eventually came closer to $600,000, but E. I. made a gift of the additional $150,000.

Along with the golf course, the clubhouse, and the swimming pool, E. I. promised to build tennis courts, to give two-thirds interest in the water company to the Club to irrigate its golf course, and to provide a family picnic ground under the oaks at the head of Lake Cascade. The Club was to be run by a board, independent of the housing development, and to have its own set of by-laws.

On August 29, 1925, the Orinda Country Club formally opened its doors to charter members and their families with picnics, luncheons, small parties, canoeing on Lake Cascade, swimming in the pool, and golf. With no road yet crossing the dam, hundreds of celebrants drove

around the lake; those arriving first parked in the single lot in front of the entrance and the others spilled out along the road. They crowded into the clubhouse and strolled down through the rose garden, in an area now paved for parking, and up to the pool.

On the golf course, only five holes (1, 15, 16, 17, and 18) were finished, so enthusiastic newcomers completed the round three times and then played 1, 15, and 18 once again. In the evening, some five hundred people attended a formal dinner dance, eating in two shifts and dancing long into the night to the music of "Puss" Donahue's band.

Originally, provision was made for 350 regular members, 500 social members, and 50 life members, with membership open only to people who purchased property in Orinda. The fees established in 1924 were $500 for a regular membership (raised to $750 by 1925), plus $10 dues per

month; $125 for social, with $5 dues per month; or $1,000 for life, with no monthly dues. The social-member category was novel, created for those who wanted to use the clubhouse, tennis court, and swimming pool but were not interested in the golf course. The founders hoped that these facilities, which often ran at a loss at similar clubs, would be profitable at Orinda. In addition, junior memberships were available to sixteen- to twenty-one-year-old children of regular members for $25, plus $3.50 dues per month, and individuals living at least fifty miles from the Club could become nonresident members for a price to be determined by the board of directors.

By the night of the grand opening, some 125 families had become members. Jimmy L'Hommedieu had been elected first president, according to the newly created by-laws; E. I. had been elected director at the first board meeting on October 28, 1924; and committees had been established to oversee finances, golf, grounds, and membership. Some 70 families lived in Orinda, 16 in homes designed by Murdock (who also designed the Club's crest), and the remainder traveled to the area to use the facilities on weekends, holidays, and vacations.

23

After completing the tenth hole, golfers in the early years cross this bridge to Miner Road en route to the eleventh tee. The bridge was constructed of concrete over pipe, simulating wood, a style used throughout the course. ◄

The Early Days

Because it was difficult at first to distinguish among the many Club members and guests, members were required to show their cards at the front desk in the 1920s before proceeding to the pool, the tennis court, or the golf shop. The back stairway did not yet exist, so they entered the golf shop by walking either around the back of the building or through the clubhouse library and out to the gardens and paths. On Sundays, the greenskeepers provided valet parking.

Those who had not yet built on their Orinda land could rent one of twelve guest rooms on the second floor of the clubhouse either by the weekend or by the month. For $40 per month, they got a room with an individual bath, electricity, heat, and a spectacular view. These people were able to enjoy parties late into the night and golf at the crack of dawn. According to Frank Brunk, Jr., whose family occupied two rooms much of one summer when he was a boy, "It was like staying in two bedrooms with a giant clubhouse as a living room."

Getting to Orinda in those days was not easy. Bob Murdock, son of Hamilton Murdock, recalls making the trip with his family:

" 'Orinda or Bust' could well have been the battle cry of those traveling from across the Berkeley-Oakland hills. The Tunnel Road was slow and dangerous. The two-lane tunnel, completed in 1901, was a narrow, wet, dripping bore with a curve near the east end that didn't belong there. The roadbed sometimes iced in winter. 'Closed for Repairs' signs were used often. . . . The road from Canary Cottage, at the east end of the tunnel, to the crossroads was as precarious as the rest of the route, with frequent slides, plenty of twists, drop-offs, and narrow bridges over long-gone sections of creek. . . . When all systems were go, this was the route to Orinda and beyond. But with no radio in those prehistoric days, one had no warning of impending delays and closures, so many took the route that was open most of the time—The Dam Road."

The Depression

In October of 1929, OCC boasted 400 regular members, 150 social members, and 20 life members. By August of 1932, the memberships had dropped to a total of 268, despite the fact that regular memberships went for $150 and social for $50. The Depression had set in throughout the country, and in the Bay Area, as everywhere else, many were no longer able to afford the luxurious living they had grown accustomed to in the 1920s. Country Club members who had purchased lots in Orinda were not able to build on them, and though some continued to make the trip over on weekends, holidays, and vacations, others withdrew their memberships altogether—Jimmy L'Hommedieu and Hamilton Murdock among them.

Many of the clubs in the area, including Diablo and Berkeley (now Mira Vista), were forced to close. At Orinda, wages for Ralph Longo, the golf professional, were cut to $75 per month, half his wages of 1928; other staff members worked twelve-hour days six days a week, with members of the greens crew, for example, making 44 cents per hour in 1933 (down from 56 cents per hour before the Depression). Lunch in the dining room cost 75 cents; a three-course dinner cost $1.

Despite the hardships, Orinda remained open. Addison Strong, president from 1936 to 1939, used his financial expertise as a certified public accountant from San Francisco to secure a bank loan and to keep the Club afloat. A new "absent" membership category was established for those who could not use the facilities but wanted to keep their memberships alive with half-rate monthly dues. Others worked out payment plans or shifted from regular to social memberships and cut back on extra activities. Those who lived in the area volunteered to work in the mornings as greenskeepers and repairmen and were able to continue golfing, swimming, riding, boating, fishing, and picnicking in the afternoons. In addition, the Club purchased equipment at bargain prices from some of the defunct area clubs and signed on some of those clubs' members. One of the few golf courses remaining open in the area, OCC scheduled fourteen tournaments in 1932.

Foreclosure was threatened more than once. Orinda's members were determined to survive, however; at one time, they offered to buy the Club, and at another, they offered to return it to E. I. But E. I. himself was in dire economic shape. The market for Haciendas homes had disappeared, and defaults on mortgages became oppressive. Economic disaster was imminent and probably would have ruined E. I. had he not previously established an honorable reputation among San Francisco bankers. Because of who he was, however, the bankers were willing to give him the time he needed to recover. He proved himself worthy of their trust when he paid off the last of his debts in the late forties after lots in Haciendas del Orinda had once again begun to sell.

By the mid-1930s, things were moving forward again. The dam on Lake Cascade was raised and El Ribero, the road across the dam, was built, creating a shortcut to Club grounds. The pool bathhouse was remodeled, modernized and doubled in size. In 1936, the Wednesday Club, a group of men who met for golf, stag dinner, and games lasting from Wednesday afternoon until Thursday morning, was organized. Often these men would

perform maintenance chores in the morning, painting and repairing the facilities and cutting the grass, for which they were rewarded with a free lunch and a glass of beer before tee time.

The completion of the Caldecott Tunnel in 1937 simplified the drive to Orinda and brought more new members. Once again the Club was a popular center of activity. The crowds became so difficult to control, in fact, that the board of directors felt it necessary to set new rules. Each member was permitted to bring no more than three guests at a time and was required to purchase a guest card at the office for 50 cents for each person to use the tennis courts or the pool. Guest green fees were set at $3 on weekends and $1.50 on weekdays.

World War II

The good times were cut short once again when the United States entered World War II in 1941. In January of 1942 forty members resigned, and in February another twenty-eight. The total numbers dropped to 142 regulars and 30 social. Again, only the determination, dedication, and innovation of Orinda's remaining members kept the Club alive. But under the leadership of Jeff Hedemark, president from 1942 to 1945, there was a spirit of camaraderie, with everyone pitching in to help maintain the facilities. Hedemark often went door to door during that time to collect back dues and inspire use of the Club.

As during the Depression, the membership was evaluated and a new category begun. This time the military itself helped save the Club. While many regular members were unable to use the facilities, Navy officers in preflight training at St. Mary's College in Moraga were anxious for the chance to relax with their families. They were pleased to be able to lease OCC memberships from regular members without paying a transfer fee and with monthly dues only half the norm;

members were equally pleased to know that their memberships would be returned to them when the war ended. Once again, as during the Depression, other country clubs—this time Berkeley (Mira Vista), Diablo, and Sequoyah—closed, and OCC purchased some of their equipment and recruited some of their members.

Also during the war years, the federal government took 20 percent of all dues to help finance the war and began taxing liquor $8 to $10 a gallon, or 12 cents a drink. Individuals attending parties were required to bring either food stamps or their own food to be served, and members carpooled to get to the Club when gasoline rationing made travel difficult. As during the Depression, members volunteered to help with maintenance and repair. Slot machines supplied by the Navy were featured in the Pine Room and also helped defray the financial burden.

With rubber going to the war effort, golf balls became scarce. Members put their names on balls so that they could be returned if lost and later found, and anyone wishing to purchase a reconditioned ball was required to turn in several used ones. Because caddies were unavailable and golfers needed to carry their own equipment, an adjustable club was

invented with one face to serve as all irons and another to serve as a putter. War bonds, nylon stockings, and spirits were given as prizes for golf tournaments, and the Spaniards vs. Indians Tournament, which had become a favorite annual event, transformed to the Spanish Navy vs. the Indian Army, with each member inviting one player from the Navy or the Army to play as a nonpaying guest.

When the war ended in the mid-1940s, memberships returned to their original owners, activities resumed, and business began growing again. With the end of gas rationing, Orinda became more accessible, and droves of people arrived. The Orinda Country Club had survived two of the most difficult times in U.S. history undamaged, making it unique among country clubs in the area. As the popularity of the Club increased, the cost of membership escalated, from $1,500 in the early 1950s to $2,500 in 1962. By 1950, some 680 families had joined the ranks. The lean times were over—for good.

29

OVERLEAF *Children line up outside the clubhouse library for OCC's first Easter egg hunt in 1925.*

PEOPLE AND PROGRAMS

The Membership

32

From the beginning, the Orinda Country Club was intended to be a family club with plenty of activities for everyone. The first women's golf group was organized in 1925, and one woman, a Berkeley High School teacher named Ida Strand, was among the first four individuals to play the completed eighteen holes. In the early years, women sold refreshments at a snack shack at the eighth hole and took wagers on who would come closest to the hole to raise money for trophies and for furnishings in their third-floor locker room.

The Women's NCGA Tournament was held at Orinda in 1928, just as the men's was, and a Women's Open Championship was held here in 1930. Women held their first invitational in 1956 and have participated in the junior-adult tournaments since 1979. In the 1980s they joined with other women of the NCGA to raise money for the Guide Dogs for the Blind Foundation, instituting an annual tournament and establishing a lending library in their locker room for contributions.

The Duffers, a nine-hole ladies' group formed in 1962, met to play each Wednesday morning; the group changed its name to the Gay-9-Tees in 1964 and to the 9-Tees in the 1980s.

Members from both ladies' groups have assisted in special men's tournaments throughout the years.

In the 1980s, a group called the Green Thumb Ladies labored to beautify the golf course, building rock gardens and planting impatiens, azaleas, rhododendrons, oleanders, and hedges.

Bridge games, often followed by fashion shows, have also been a favorite activity for women throughout the years.

34

"Being a junior member at Orinda was much like being a full member, but with no bills to pay," writes Bob Murdock of his experience here in the 1920s. "No other club I've heard of was ever more kind and thoughtful to its juniors."

The first junior golf championships at Orinda were held as early as 1926 and 1927, with the first father-son tournament in 1933. Golf Pro Pat Patten began Saturday clinics in the late 1940s to teach OCC youth both the techniques and the etiquette of the game. The first Wally Riddell Junior Trophy for good sportsmanship, now given annually, was awarded in 1982. In 1983, OCC won special recognition when members Mike Fabian and Brian McDonnell placed first and second respectively in the NCGA Junior Championship; it was the first time that a single club had produced both of the top winners. Since 1990, children ages six to eight have been able to get an early start in the sport through the Club's Little Linkers program.

The swimming facilities have been another popular site for juniors throughout the years, starting in the 1920s, when the girls in particular would sit around the pool reading and listening to phonograph records—Bing Crosby was a favorite—on their Victrola players. The first swim meet, held in 1935 against Diablo and Claremont country clubs, was a great success, with Orinda coming out the winner. Swim races, diving competitions, and the Aquacades—a program of synchronized swimming performed by the older girls each summer between 1947 and 1961—have all been popular, as have lessons for the younger children.

A junior tennis program begun in the 1950s has been a more recent hit with the young ones. The Easter Vacation Tournament for high-school tennis players was a highlight in the late 1950s and 1960s. Participants in the OCC Grand Prix, instituted in 1984, accumulate points based on participation throughout the summer as they compete for trophies awarded at the end of the season. And at summer tennis camp, first introduced in 1988, youngsters ages nine to seventeen take part in intensive league and ladder competition with individual attention from one instructor for every three players. The one-week sessions always fill long before summer arrives.

E. I. himself began the tradition in the 1920s of hosting an annual Easter egg hunt for the youngsters, a favorite event for many OCC families. The first hunts were held in the rose garden above and around the pool area. After finding their eggs, the children would be entertained with games; a sack-race winner was awarded a live bunny. Because of the large number of sign-ups, the event was moved to the sixteenth and seventeenth fairways in 1962, where it has taken place since, with magicians and clowns for entertainment. Today the men play an Easter tournament on sixteen holes instead of eighteen to give priority to the children.

In the early years, Sunday dinners were frequently family events followed by sing-alongs. Teen dances began in 1961, with a $2.50 per person fee for dinner, dancing, and entertainment. A family picnic day on the eighteenth fairway in August; a father-daughter dinner-dance around Valentine's Day; a father-son sports-dinner; a Christmas breakfast with Santa Claus and gifts (replacing an earlier afternoon sing-along with Santa)—all are annual events enjoyed by hundreds of children since the early years at OCC.

36

Seniors at Orinda have been active for many years, with a new membership category designated in 1970 for those over seventy-one years of age. In 1976, they began driving from gold markers with senior NCGA ratings. A special golfing event for the Club's senior members is the Squires Invitational held each fall; home-and-home tournaments with other clubs are also held throughout the year.

Those interested in tennis can participate in the Northern California-sanctioned Senior Tennis Tournament held at Orinda each year. In the 1980s, another tournament held for both men and women combined golf and tennis scores of competing seniors.

The Squires

Nature

Among the things that most attracted E. I. deLaveaga to Orinda from the start was its wild lands for hunting and fishing. San Pablo Creek, filled with trout and salmon, delighted him even in his boyhood. For several years during the 1920s an annual fishing derby at Lake Cascade marked the opening of trout season, usually the first weekend in May. E. I. would ride up on his beautiful white horse, dressed in handsome white leathers, to start the activities. At the end of the day, when all fishing had ended, awards were given for the first fish caught, the largest fish caught, and the most fish caught, with prizes going to men, women, and children; then the catch was barbecued and served at a picnic for all participants.

Also advocating E. I.'s love of the land, a nature trail circled Lake Cascade in the 1920s. The Sierra Club of Berkeley published a booklet with the names of the wildlife along the trail, both flora and fauna, and with descriptions of the small animals and birds to be seen while hiking. Since 1914, the area had been used as a bird sanctuary, with 178 known species, including brown and rufous-sided towhees, red-shafted flickers, horned owls, and mockingbirds. After publication of the Sierra Club booklet, on the advice of UC Davis, OCC members

helped in an attempt to import every known plant variety that would survive in the region's climate and soil conditions around the lake and the golf course. They planted more than fourteen hundred new trees, including specimens of Port Orford cedar, Arizona cypress, Colorado blue spruce, wild lilac, and mulberry. After the Club was established, E. I. won many ribbons at the county fair in Martinez for the roses he grew in the garden in the area now paved for the lower parking lot.

In addition, sixteen miles of horse trails wound throughout Haciendas del Orinda when the Club opened in the 1920s. Although the Club did not have stables on its grounds, members and property owners were lured to Miss Graham's Riding Academy with generous discounts that allowed them to ride for $1 for the first hour and for 50 cents for each hour thereafter.

E. I. deLaveaga returns from a successful hunting trip, a favorite pastime of his since boyhood. ◄

The Clubhouse

The OCC clubhouse—perched at the top of a cliff of natural rock and overlooking the Club's eighteenth fairway and the San Pablo Valley below—was something to be proud of when it opened its doors in 1925. Stately in the Spanish Mediterranean style of Hamilton Murdock, it boasted a low-pitched roof covered with curved red tile, balconies, archways, grillwork of decorative wrought iron, textured stucco exteriors, and wooden shutters. When construction of the building began in 1924, the cost was estimated at $80,000; by the time it was completed in 1925, something closer to $214,000 had been invested, including the costs of furnishing.

Originally the building housed a lobby; a dining room (the Orinda Room); a library (the passageway between the Fairway Lounge and the lobby), filled with books and magazines about golf and likened to the Bancroft Library at UC Berkeley; a porch (now the terrace dining area); and kitchen facilities. Large glass doors opened from the library onto the wide porch running the length of the building, a patio, and two paths, one leading to the rose garden and the pool and the other to the first tee and the golf shop. The building's elegant archways, balconies, and high ceilings of ornate walnut and mahogany were all part of the Spanish decor. On the second floor were guest rooms for rent by members and friends of members, and on the third floor were office space, rooms for employees, and the women's locker room, now the groom's room for weddings.

Through the years, the clubhouse has seen a number of changes. The Pine Room, the original bar, was added in the early 1930s, immediately after Prohibition ended, financed by members' contributions. In 1951, a new, enlarged men's grill and bar opened. Then, in 1961, plans were made for a new cocktail lounge, a new ladies' locker room with restrooms

on the first floor, upstairs offices, redecoration of the dining terrace, and modernization of the entryway. The most ambitious of these, the Fairway Lounge, was completed in 1962. The men's grill and showers were enlarged in 1965, and in 1966, a large covered porch was built adjacent to the men's grill.

More recent major changes, in the early 1980s, included, among other things, the construction of a new parking lot where E. I.'s rose garden had once been and the conversion of the covered porch to the Oak Room for dining, with kitchen improvements on the lower level. While construction interrupted kitchen activities, the Cascade Room became the pantry for light lunches served in the Fairway Lounge, and the porch terrace became the men's grill for cards and dominoes.

The city of Orinda honored OCC in 1988 when it requested that the clubhouse be designated a historical landmark.

THE MANAGEMENT

Management has always played an important role in OCC operations, often helping to set the tone of the Club. In the beginning, managers came and went: first the Nielson couple, who rented a house across the lake from the Club; then Edwin Cooper; then, in the early 1930s, Mary Gallagher. When Gallagher resigned in 1935, the popular caddy master, Joe Varney, took her place.

Here for the long term, though, was the well-loved Clarke Mathews, who first worked a stint from 1944 to 1948 and then returned in 1950 for twenty more years. Mathews came to the Club from San Francisco's Palace Hotel and brought with him a following of loyal and dedicated staffpersons, mostly Filipinos, some who remained for several decades. Called Mr. Hospitality, he would greet people by first name at the clubhouse entrance. Mathews persuaded the Club to hire maitre d' Alec Churchward as his successor in 1970. Since 1989, Keith Melton has held the position; he now manages a staff of some fifty employees.

Also in 1944, George Kropf joined the staff as chief engineer. He came to OCC from the Heinz Company in Berkeley and found more than "fifty-seven varieties" of jobs to do at the Club, including renovating the pool area, repairing the clubhouse, and building bridges.

PROHIBITION
AND SLOTS

The original clubhouse lobby exemplifies Hamilton Murdock's Spanish Mediterranean style with its lavish height, interior balconies, carved wooden ceilings, and wrought iron light fixtures. ▶

Bartender Benny presides over the Club's first bar, the Pine Room, built immediately after Prohibition ended in 1933.

Because the clubhouse was constructed during the era of Prohibition, it originally included no bar. This did not prevent the flow of alcohol, however. No such law could dampen the spirits at OCC, where members felt insulated from Contra Costa's county seat, faraway Martinez, and where influential members could give early warnings of pending county inspections. Liquor seemed always to be in plentiful supply, provided in locker rooms by the medical men of the Club and hidden in a clubhouse dumbwaiter.

Alcohol was not the only forbidden fruit enjoyed at OCC during the jovial twenties. Slot machines, too, were popular. Like alcohol, these machines were to be hidden in the dumbwaiter if word should ever come of a county inspection. For more than two and a half years, the slots prevailed, bringing the Club revenues of some $2,000 a month. The spoils would have been double that, except that half went to the county in accordance with an agreement between the Club and the county controller of the time, who was a golfing friend of an Orinda member.

As soon as Prohibition ended, OCC members determined to build a bar in their beloved clubhouse. Financed through voluntary contributions and built by members, the Pine Room—so named because of the wallpaper of pine boughs—opened in the 1930s, complete with its mahogany bar. To the disappointment of many members, the bar was removed when kitchen renovations became necessary. The room is still used for private parties, board meetings, and other social events, however.

CLUBHOUSE
ACTIVITIES

In addition to dining and attending parties at the clubhouse, members have used the facilities for a variety of more sedentary activities. Bridge playing has always been popular here, with contract bridge held Thursday nights, preceded by a $1 dinner in the 1930s. Luncheons followed by bridge, often accompanied by fashion shows, became a regular part of women's social activities beginning in 1946 and continuing into the 1980s. A new twist, the bridge marathon, began in 1987, with each team playing against a different team every month from September through May and with the overall winner announced at a luncheon. From time to time, couples have met one night a month to play bridge, sometimes with dinner and always with a kitty going to the winner. Meanwhile, the men have played cards and dominoes in the grill for years, with domino tournaments beginning in 1961.

At the first OCC art fair in September of 1965, all members were invited to bring paintings, crafts, and jewelry for display. Forty-one members contributed, and two hundred attended the opening. The event was so popular that it was repeated. In the early 1970s, a committee judged which of five items submitted per member would be hung. By the mid-1970s, the fair had become so successful that a continuous exhibit was instigated, with the works of a different person displayed in the Cascade Room each month or two.

Rattan chairs and Japanese paper lanterns ornament the terrace dining room of 1924. From here, spectators would watch the play at the final hole during tournaments. ◄

Golf

48

The Orinda Country Club's golf course was given as an example of one of the finest early American courses in *The Links,* a popular book about golf-course design published in 1926 by Robert Hunter, who had traveled extensively and studied the great courses of England and Scotland. One famous picture from Orinda's fifteenth tee appears in that book with a favorable comparison to the *Redan,* the fifteenth hole at North Burwick, Scotland, the most famous par three in all of golf at the time. Like the best Scottish courses, Orinda's course has dogleg holes and depends more on natural hazards than on traps and artificially constructed troublemakers. Its five doglegs, its narrow, tree-lined, sloping fairways, and its blind shots make it particularly difficult.

The building of the golf course in the 1920s was a great endeavor, requiring more than three years and costing just over $59,000. Only the first five holes were completed in time for the Club's 1925 opening. Soon after, the Cardiac Nine—holes 1, 2, 3, and 13 through 18, named for the largely flat terrain—were completed; the entire course was finally ready for play in 1927, just in time for the NCGA tournament the next spring. With a few exceptions, the course remains much today as it was when Watson designed it.

Building the course was highly labor-intensive. Humans, horses, and mules did all the work of grading, scraping, and digging the original farmland with the aid of only two small tractors. Changing the landscape as little as necessary, the workers bared, covered, rolled, and seeded the ground; they carved walking paths out of hillsides, tucked tees among trees, constructed greens along the valley's natural contours.

Maintenance in the twenties was also a mammoth chore. During those early years, sheep were used to keep the rough down where machines could not do the job. Greenskeepers spent about ten hours every night watering the course, pulling out hundred-foot lengths of one-inch-diameter hose. Often they had to stop work to extract small fish from the nozzles and the sprinkler heads. In the spring, they would perforate the greens with a pitchfork and then spread a dressing over the top, pulling a crude horizontal bar with vertical teeth from one side to the other to even out the surface. It took an employee a full day to walk the course and change the holes on each green.

In the end, the work paid off. According to a December 1927 issue of *The Fairway* magazine: "No more beautiful setting could be asked for an inland course. Fine big oaks line the fairways and guard the greens. The course bends around the base of the hills and extends up the canyons toward the club-house. Watson has made the best of an excellent opportunity. . . . The last five holes are perhaps the most beautiful and picturesque golf holes of any inland course in the country—great old spreading oak trees surrounded with fine verdant turf—landscaping that satisfies and makes you enjoy your game even though you are playing badly."

Altogether, the course was 6,315 yards long, with four par fives, ten par fours, and four par threes: a total par of seventy-two. Six times it crossed the Lauterwasser Creek, twice the San Pablo Creek, and twice the remains of the Cascade Creek, which had once flowed down the middle of the eighteenth fairway.

Following Scottish custom, Willie Watson was instrumental in naming each of the holes at Orinda, though these names were not officially designated until 1927. Reflecting the area's geography, its Indian and Spanish heritage, and the Scottish tradition, the names are as follows:

The first hole was called *Inspiration* because of its magnificent view. The original tee was where the back parking lot is presently, about thirty feet higher and directly to the right of the current first tee; the hole was even more of a blind shot then than it is now. From a lookout post to the left of the tee, one could see a forecaddy or a golf-shop employee, who would signal an okay for a first tee shot. At the original tee were also a small practice green and some benches. Frequently an audience would gather to watch the beginning of a match. The tee was moved to its current location in 1952, at which time the original caddy yard there became a practice green.

The second hole was called *Bonita*, Spanish for beautiful. Originally the green was some 120 feet from front to back; a new bunker and green were constructed in 1932 with a sand trap at the right front. A periscope installed in 1945 allowed the golfer to judge the distance of the players ahead prior to teeing off. The fairway slope has since been leveled to increase visibility and the periscope removed.

The third hole was *Orchard*, named for the old pear orchard on both sides of the fairway, dating back to the time when the property had belonged to the deLaveaga family and had been planted as a fruit orchard.

Fourth was *Meteor*, named for the rocks above the green. Old-timers say this was the most difficult green to construct because the solid rock on which it was built had to be covered with soil in order for grass to grow there. The sand traps originally in front of the green were removed and left as rough in 1932. A new sand trap was added on the uphill fairway in 1989.

The fifth hole, named *Mousetrap*, is a tricky dogleg between the land and the creek on one side and Miner Road, out-of-bounds, on the other. A swale at the green was constructed in 1928 to add an extra challenge for NCGA tournament competitors.

Following Scottish tradition, the sixth hole, the longest of the course (originally 557 yards), is named *Longtom*. The golfer's tee shot must cross Miner Road and dogleg left onto the fairway. From the beginning, this has been the number-one handicap hole. Additional mounds and sand traps have been added around the green.

Sobrante, the seventh hole, was named after the street running alongside it. Its tee was originally located in a higher position than it is today; the golfer climbed a

The first men's foursome to play the eighteen-hole course after its completion in 1927 tee off at the eighth hole.

51

flight of steps from the sixth green to the tee area and looked out on a beautiful view. The tee was cut down in 1952 and the dirt moved to fill a cavern in front of the eleventh tee.

Deadhorse, the name of the eighth and shortest hole (originally 123 yards), is a derivation of Dead Horse Gulch, the name of the area in which one of deLaveaga's horses had died. The grass between the tee and the traps was taken out in 1932 to eliminate maintenance problems; later, with sprinkling systems installed, it was replanted.

Because the ninth fairway had once been used by the deLaveagas for their stable and polo matches, this hole was named *Horseshoe*. In 1932, the fairway was narrowed at the entry of the green. A mirror on a high pole installed behind the tee in 1978 allows players to see when those in the group ahead have hit their second shots.

The tenth hole, from which one can look down the fairway on a delightful scene, is named *Delight*. The name is not for the view, however, but in honor of E. I.'s wife, also named Delight. With Lauterwasser Creek to the right and out-of-bounds to the left, the golfer must hit a straight shot to approach the small green banked by

A golfer makes a fairway shot to the eleventh green at Graveyard, *the site of an old Indian burial ground.*

52

sand traps. The deLaveaga home off Miner Road adjoins this fairway.

The eleventh hole, named *Graveyard*, is at the site of an old Indian burial ground discovered in 1924 when artifacts, including stone utensils, were unearthed during construction of the golf course. The Costanoan Indians, inhabitants of Contra Costa County from at least five thousand years ago until the early 1900s, disposed of food and buried their dead in what might today be called a dump. Some of the artifacts found in this area may now be seen at UC Berkeley's Kroeber Museum. In his efforts to retain the character of the original landscape, Watson designed this fairway with grassy mounds to replace the original burial grounds; the approach shots here are as tricky as if they were through sand traps. A snack shack was constructed here in 1951, and a cavern in front of the tee was filled with dirt taken from the seventh hole in 1952.

Marie deLaveaga, Miguel's wife, masterminded the building of Santa Maria Chapel across Miner Road from the eleventh green. Patterned after a country church she had visited in France as a little girl, the chapel was dedicated in October 1896. Marie had worked hard to make it a reality—perhaps too hard, as the baby she was carrying at the time was born dead and she herself died a few days after the dedication. Mass was held here every other Sunday until 1914, when Miguel died and the funds for the services ceased. Services were continued from the 1930s until 1955, when a new church was built and this site sold.

Following another tradition from Scotland, the twelfth hole was named to honor the course architect, *Willie Watson*. This fairway was leveled in 1961 to prevent blind shots to the green. A new sand trap on the right fairway since 1989 makes a golfer's tee shot more demanding.

To understand the meaning of the name of the thirteenth hole, *Mokelumne*, it is necessary to understand something of the area's water system. The water at the East Bay Municipal Utility District's filter plant on Camino Pablo originates from the Mokelumne River in the Sierra Nevada and travels to the plant through underground tunnels beneath Highway 24, Orinda's Charles Hill area, private property, and the golf course. In the Sierra, before it makes its way to Orinda, the Mokelumne is also the source of the Blue Hole, the inspiration for the original waterfall carrying water from Lake Cascade to the OCC pool. Nine workmen for the water company were killed by a huge cave-in while constructing the tunnel beneath this hole. A second sand trap was added to the left of the green in 1928 to make the hole more challenging for competitors in the NCGA tournament.

Ralph Longo, Orinda's first golf pro, drives from the fifteenth tee.

54

The fourteenth hole, *San Pablo*, is bordered on the right by San Pablo Creek. Although this is a short hole, the narrow green and deep sand traps make it a tricky par four. During World War II, when military personnel stationed at St. Mary's College leased Club memberships (before the pine trees along the creek had been planted), a Catholic chaplain scored an ace here. Fairway sand traps were added in 1989.

The fifteenth hole, made famous by Robert Hunter in *The Links*, is named *Despair* because it is surrounded by trouble. The hole, originally 173 yards long, crosses the San Pablo Creek. Here golfers in the early days were known to fish for their dinner before completing a game. The major widening of Camino Pablo in 1958 reduced the fringe area between the green and the out-of-bounds fence.

I AM THE FIFTEENTH GREEN

Propped against the glow of the setting sun I boldly defy the gods of golf and the mashies of men.

With ghoulish glee I fling into the depths of the ditch that guards me, or hide in the hellish heel-print left in the sizzling sands that border my base, shots that would pierce my bulging bosom.

Captains of Industry, Builders of Railroads, Conquerors of Trade, Masters of Men, shake and shiver as they approach ME because I am unapproachable.

Devotees of the Ancient and Honorable from all walks of life woo me with soft words and prayerful pleadings, but I hear them not.

E'en to the charms of the lovely ladies of Orinda I am adamant.

Men with the form of an Ayton, the finesse of an Evans, the rhythm of a Vardon and the wallop of a Ray descend the steps to the Sixteenth Tee with bowed heads and heavy hearts because I have robbed them of their birthright—a par 3.

Sired by the Devil of Devils, born under the star of Evil, and nurtured by the Mother of Despair, I wreck men's souls; I kill their hopes; I muss up their scores; I make them late for dinner.

Though they curse and revile me, I laugh at their epithets and mock their impotent efforts to conquer me.

I am the unconquered and the unconquerable.

I AM THE FIFTEENTH GREEN.

Robert B. Johnson
1928

Golfers in the 1920s tee off the first hole from a location about thirty feet higher and to the right of today's first tee. From the lookout post, they could see when the fairway was clear before they began their round.

The sixteenth hole, named *Gibralter* (meaning rock wall), has the tee area built on rock. The Pacific Gas and Electric tower and wires in the middle of this fairway have provoked much discussion through the years as Orinda has considered moving the tower to the area between the sixteenth and seventeenth fairways. For economic reasons, the move has never been made.

Rincon, the name of the seventeenth hole, is Spanish for cozy corner. This is a fitting name for the old entrance to the deLaveaga subdivision of Haciendas del Orinda as golfers turn the corner and head toward the finishing holes.

Finally, the eighteenth hole, *Cascade*, named for the creek that had once flowed down its fairway, is a magnificent and challenging 510-yard par five. Before deLaveaga built the Country Club, the California Nevada Railroad crossed this fairway on its journey from Emeryville through Richmond, up the San Pablo Valley to the Bryant Station located south of Highway 24 near Orinda Theater Square. The railroad was intended to go all the way to Livermore, Nevada, and even Utah, but it never got past Orinda. It was a primary mode of transportation for the deLaveaga family before it was discontinued at the turn of the century. Because the trains could not turn around, they backed all the way to Emeryville on the return trip.

With the coming of gas golf carts in the 1960s, asphalt paths were built throughout the course, and the original bridges, constructed of wood-simulating concrete, were replaced by wider, laminated bridges that more readily accommodate carts and maintenance equipment. Much of the course was fenced in the early seventies to protect it from joggers, trespassers, and poachers, and to prevent vandalism. Automatic sprinklers were first installed in 1966; more recently, a computerized system was installed in 1988. And beautification projects through the years have included the planting of trees and flowers and the installation of attractive wooden signs.

A new rating from the NCGA in 1989 gave the course a 73 for women, 70 for men, 68.5 for seniors, and 71 from the championship tees. With all its changes, it is now a total of 6,127 yards long, virtually the same yardage as when originally constructed.

THE GAME

In recalling the 1920s game of golf at the Orinda Country Club, Bob Murdock wrote: "My memories of Orinda Country Club always start with the thrill of driving from the old first tee. All the world seemed to be at one's feet. . . . Located under what is now the end of the parking lot, the tee area was itself a gem. With several oaks to cast their shadows, a small putting green for those waiting to tee off, and flowered landscaping and several benches, this was a grand place to gather on a Sunday afternoon."

Golf in the 1920s was similar to what it is today—an invigorating day with friends on the course. But any observer then and now would quickly note some differences. Then, before the advent of television, spectators would gather on the first tee to see the start of a game; they would also line the clubhouse balcony or stand on the decks below the lower tennis courts to watch the play at the final hole.

In the 1920s, golf attire for males consisted of knickers or plus fours, sleeveless argyle sweaters, and argyle knee socks held up with tassels. Ties and jackets were also required of players off the first tee, but many a golfer would strip down after sinking the first ball and stash his formal wear on a rock or a tree limb, to be retrieved later at the eighteenth tee. Ladies wore full-length skirts, large hats, and hose.

Golf clubs were not numbered then but rather were named. The woods were *driver*, *brassie*, *spoon*, and *cleek*; the irons were *iron-cleek* (or *driving-iron*), *mid-iron*, *mid-mashie*, *mashie*, *spade-mashie*, *mashie-niblick*, and *niblick*; and the putter was called a *jigger*. Balls were all white, quick to turn dingy, and expensive. At a time when the price of a sumptuous prime rib dinner was $2.50, a single ball cost 50 cents.

At each tee in the 1920s, two buckets hung from hooks on an iron A-frame. One contained water, the other sand. In turn, each golfer would take a handful of sand, dip it into the water to give it some body, and make a mound of it on which to place the ball. These buckets were replaced by ball washers after wooden tee markers came into use in 1936. Today golfers find buckets containing grass seed and fertilizer for repairing divots on some tees.

The game has changed little through the years, with two important exceptions. First, there was no imbedded ball rule in 1920: A plugged ball had to be hacked out. Second, there *was* such a thing as a stymie. If one player's ball blocked another's path, the options were to go over or around it. The United States Golfing Association did allow relief if one ball was closer than six inches to another or if it was closer than six inches to the hole (thus the tradition of having six-inch-long scorecards), but Scottish and Royal and Ancient regulations did not permit even this. Jake Schaefer, world billiard champion and an OCC member, frequently won matches by jumping his ball over an opponent's when sinking a putt.

Orinda's second golf pro, Pat Patten (left), meets with 1942 OCC President Jeff Hedemark.

60

It is a tribute to the appeal of Orinda that the Club has had only three golf pros throughout its history: Ralph Longo, from 1924 to 1942; Pat Patten, until 1973; and Ray Orr, through 1991.

Leaving a prior position as assistant golf pro at the Claremont Country Club and taking the challenge of working at a new club where many of the members were initially strangers to one another, Longo set the tone for OCC by encouraging a spirit of friendship among golfers. With no professional tournaments to lure him away in those days, he remained close to home and contributed greatly to the development and organization of the Club's early tournaments. After leaving here in 1942, he went to Golden Gate Fields to complete a sixty-three-year golfing career. At the time, he had given the longest continuous service for any golf pro in any club in California.

The Club's second pro, Pat Patten, was equally devoted, congenial, friendly, and knowledgeable. He participated in World War II efforts to teach golf to returning soldiers at Oak Knoll Navy Rehabilitation Hospital, taught young and old, and wrote monthly golf highlights in *The Orindan*'s "Pat's Plaudits." Even while serving a term as president of the Northern California Professional Golf Association from 1949 to 1952, he found plenty of time for giving lessons and providing services to the folks at home. Among his accomplishments was the beginning of free children's classes, including instruction on everything from the proper swing to proper etiquette and the conditions of play. He also fought for the enlargement and modernization of the golf shop in the mid-1960s. Many old members returned for Patten's retirement dinner, and other professionals spoke. For his years of service, the Club gave him a trip to Scotland (where he had never been), a life membership, and a hole-in-one trophy (because, despite all his fine playing, he had never scored a hole in one).

Ray Orr, OCC's third pro, began at the Country Club as a caddy; he lived in the

Ray Orr advanced from golf caddy to OCC's third golf pro during his forty-five years with the Club.

61

Golf pro Pat Patten assists members of the UC Berkeley golf team in the 1950s. ▶

Frank McCann posted the lowest official recorded score at OCC. ▼

MEN					HOLE		WOMEN	
PAR	YDS	HDP					HDP	PAR
4	330	17	3		1	4	13	4
4	315	11	4		2	3	3	4
3	243	5	3		3	3	15	3
5	455	13	4		4	4	7	5
4	378	7	4		5	4	5	4
5	558	3	4		6	5	1	5
4	316	9	4		7	3	11	4
3	117	15	3		8	3	17	3
4	429	1	4		9	5	9	5
36	3141		33		OUT	34		37
4	304	10	3		10	4	14	4
4	447	2	4		11	5	2	5
5	451	18	4		12	4	6	5
3	171	14	2		13	3	18	3
4	295	12	3		14	4	12	4
3	166	8	3		15	3	16	3
4	405	4	4		16	4	4	4
4	343	16	4		17	3	10	4
5	521	6	4		18	5	8	5
36	3103		31		IN	35		37
72	6244		33		TOTAL	34		74
DATE	8/16/54	64			HDP	69		
					NET			

SCORER   ATTEST

community and first applied for a position as a ten-year-old but was turned away that year because the bags were bigger than he was. Orr joined the ranks the following year, in 1947. In 1960, he became assistant pro and caddy master, and in January of 1974 he advanced to pro. Among his contributions to the Club was his initiation of foreign travel, with the first trip to Portugal in 1973, followed by later ventures to Hong Kong, Great Britain, Spain, and Australia and through the Panama Canal. Another contribution has been his 1975 introduction of the annual Pro-Am Tournament, when professionals from Northern California bring one club friend each and form a team with three Orinda members. Orr also held spring classes for Orinda's women and supervised the junior golf program. He retired at the end of 1991.

Keeping enough pleasant and competent caddies to help on the hilly terrain at Orinda before carts came into vogue was always a challenge. The trip to Orinda from anywhere in the Bay Area was long and difficult, and when a young boy did arrive, he could not be certain that he would have a job. The most skilled caddy in the 1920s was able to earn 75 cents per loop per bag—a possible $3 plus tips for two double loops—if he was lucky.

Largely because of the efforts of the Club's first caddy master, Joe Varney, early golfers here were able to get the caddy services they needed. Varney, also chief of the Orinda Volunteer Fire Department, loved people of all ages and organized many activities for residents of Orinda. He was barbecue chef after the early fishing derbies and ran the fireworks shows over Lake Cascade on the Fourth of July. After proving himself as a temporary Club manager when the former manager, Mary Gallagher, resigned in 1935, Varney took the job in 1936. He eventually received a lifetime Club membership in appreciation of his many fine services.

The caddy shack in the 1920s was located below the present practice green. Varney spent many hours training the young boys to be caddies and rated them for their capabilities and knowledge. C-level caddies were novices; Bs were learning; and As, who received pins to signify their status, were the highest achievers. Pay ranged from 25 cents to 75 cents per round, depending on the caddy's ranking. Ladies' Day, every Friday morning, was an especially big day. The women, in their long skirts and hose, were always thankful for assistants to carry their bags and scramble down steep creek slopes to retrieve balls.

"Straight Down the Middle" Bing Crosby (right) visits Orinda Country Club during the 1960s to play in one of Don Doten's Sports Institute tournaments.

The New York Yankees' immortal "Joltin' Joe" DiMaggio (left) joins with Orinda's Pat Patten at an annual Doten tournament.

As part of his efforts to keep the needed caddies happy, Varney started a caddy tournament in 1928, with a hundred caddies competing and enjoying entertainment, boxing matches, and sing-a-longs afterward. In another effort to make the job fun, he directed the production of a show in 1933 called *Priscilla Takes Up Golf,* in which each caddy mimicked or ridiculed one OCC member with notorious habits. This was probably the first *Orinda Foolies.*

The need for caddies began to dwindle in the early sixties when the first gas carts arrived at Orinda. By the eighties, the caddies were rare. Those who did work earned $10 per round for a single bag and had to be reserved in the golf shop. Today caddies are virtually extinct, except for forecaddies during big tournaments. Originally the Club leased twelve three-wheeled carts, but they were too dangerous on Orinda's terrain. Today fifty-two four-wheeled electric carts are in service.

Through the years, Orinda has hosted a number of top personalities. Don Doten's Sports Institute, with annual tournaments at Orinda during the 1960s to raise money for the local Boys' Club, brought in several big names, including Bing

his victory in the 1964 British Open; he drove the tenth green at Orinda with a three-wood and sank his putt for an eagle. Bobby Jones, Jack Benny, Bob Hope, Patty Berg, Harold "Jug" McSpaden, and Byron Nelson all played here as well, some of them practicing at Orinda before participating in the January Crosby in Monterey. Singer John Raitt entertained in the Fairway Lounge after one tournament.

Orinda has also produced a few top players of its own. Bill Higgins was National Senior Amateur Champion in his first entry in the 1960s. Two of the best-known Orinda golfers, Tom Telfer and Barbara "Bobbie" Dawson, shared the distinction of winning both the Orinda and Claremont championships, Telfer in 1933 and Dawson in 1949. Telfer also won the Northern California Amateur Tournament in 1933 and was president of the NCGA in 1935 and 1936 and of the California Golf Association in 1937. He served on the Executive Committee of the U.S. Golf Association from 1937 to 1942. Dawson qualified for the U.S. Women's Amateur in 1948.

Crosby, Joe DiMaggio, Ken Venturi, Johnny Weissmuller, and Harvie Ward, two-time national amateur champion. In his initial tournament at Orinda, Ward birdied the first, second, and third holes, and turned in a low gross score of 65. On another outing he eagled the tenth and seventeenth holes with perfect wedge shots to the green. Fred Waring played a round here with a complete set of all woods. "Champagne" Tony Lema brought and displayed his trophy from

Orinda Country Club member Tom Telfer was one of OCC's premier golfers.

The first mixed-couples tournament was played at Orinda in 1925, when only five holes had been completed. Joe Varney organized it to interest more people in the sport and to lure people to the Orinda area. He and his partner, E. I.'s daughter, Lucia, won the tournament, but they graciously awarded the silver tray prize to the second-place winners.

With eighteen holes barely completed, Orinda hosted the NCGA amateur championship in 1928. The tournament that year was a departure from what it had been in the past. Claude Faw, then OCC's Green chair, lobbied for opening the championship to any NCGA member with a handicap of fifteen or lower. As a result, more than 250 golfers—rather than the usual 80 or 90—qualified. Faw also saw that members of the press were treated royally, given a room with a telephone for each reporter and provided with lunch and general hospitality. Largely as a result of his efforts, the publicity was extensive and OCC earned a place on the map.

The event was memorable. The eventual champion, an unknown seventeen-year-

old from San Francisco's Presidio Club, Lawson Little, Jr., won against a field of thirty-three tournament players—after hitting an ace at the eighth hole during the semifinals. As luck would have it, a photographer with a large, noisy camera happened to shoot the very play that made history for Little, a distraction that infuriated the youth before he realized what he had done. Having launched his career, Little went on to become one of the premier professional golfers of his time and to win the U.S. Open in 1940.

The men's championship winner in 1928, Stuart Hawley, Jr., was also young, a sixteen-year-old member of the junior group who was permitted to enter the tournament because of his low handicap. The women's NCGA tournament that year, with a $2.50 entry fee, brought thirty-eight participants.

Always a popular event at Orinda, the Fourth of July Tournament was first held in 1926 with an entry fee of $2.50 for members or $5 for nonmembers. Dinner and fireworks over the lake followed the tournament. In the early years, qualifying rounds were played on July 4, with additional rounds concluding a week later. Initially everyone began on the first tee. Calcutta bids on teams made this tournament's prizes very profitable. The format changed to two-man better ball in 1955.

67

Spectators gather at the fourth green during a Club championship tournament. ◄

68

In 1977, a shotgun tournament was introduced. This three-day event is renowned in Northern California golf circles, with a practice round and stag dinner, a women's tournament, and a concluding dinner-dance.

Also dating back to the 1920s was a New Year's Day Tournament. Following a New Year's Eve dinner-dance that might last until 4 A.M. and then breakfast, the heartiest of golfers—with few caddies to assist them—would trudge down to the course with bags, clubs, balls, and booze.

Another popular tournament was the Spaniards vs. Indians. The first such contest was in 1928, with sixty-six entries. That year Warren Harold, president of the Orinda Improvement Association and a member of OCC, instigated Fiesta Week to show pride in the Spanish background of the area. All participants wore fiesta attire and attended a dinner-dance at OCC after the festivities concluded.

For the tournament, members from one side of the men's locker room were Spanish Barons; those from the other were Indian Chiefs. The losers—until 1938, always the Chiefs—bought dinner. In 1942, the locker-room rivalry ended and the Indian Princes (new members) competed against the Spanish Barons (older members). During the war years, the Spanish Navy competed against the Indian Army, with each member encouraged to invite one member of the Navy or Army as playing guests. The tradition faded after the War, to be revived one last time for the Golden Anniversary celebration in 1974.

Other popular tournaments have joined the ranks through the years. The annual Tournament of Champions, with the name of each year's winner placed on the Tom Telfer trophy displayed in the showcase of the clubhouse lobby, began in 1976. All OCC tournament winners for the year participate. In the Big Game Tournament, OCC members who are UC Berkeley alumni have competed against Stanford alums since 1977. The Willie Watson Tournament, starting with a breakfast of Scottish eggs, kippers, and scones, finds golfers wearing knickers, ties, and other Scottish fashions. Prizes

Spanish Barons competed against
Indian Chiefs in popular Spanish vs.
Indian tournaments in the 1920s,
1930s, and 1940s.

for both golf and attire include bottles of
scotch. Bagpipers provide atmosphere
throughout the tournament, which
began in 1985. The golf-and-tennis tournaments, testing the dual skills of participants, began in 1987—as did the Jeff
Hedemark Memorial Tournament for
parent-offspring teams.

The UC Berkeley golf team, which
has used the OCC course since 1928,
hosted the Pac-Ten Championship here
in 1988. Since the seventies, Miramonte
and Campolindo high schools have
used the course for their teams' practices
and matches.

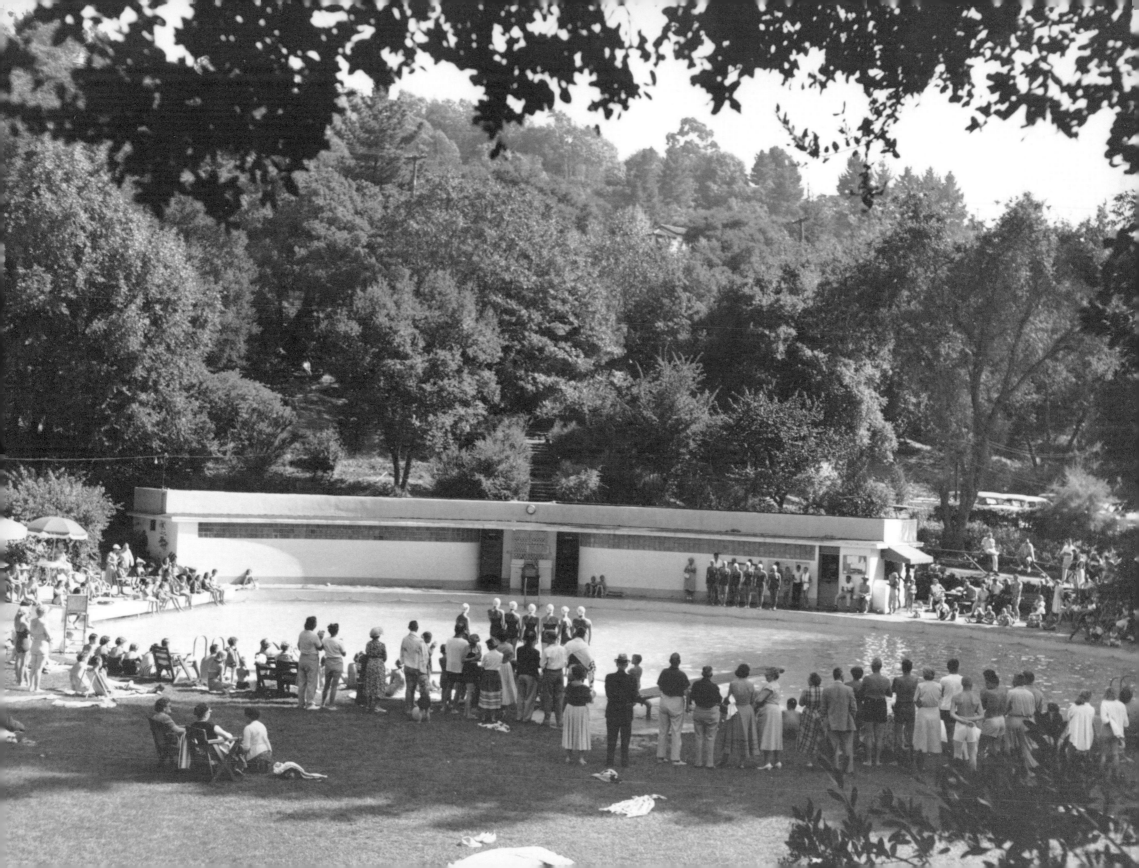

Swimming

The largest free-form swimming pool in the Bay Area when it was completed in 1924, the Orinda Country Club's earliest attraction remains a highlight for many members, particularly the younger ones. Originally, a thirty-five-foot waterfall surrounded by rocks carried water from Lake Cascade to the pondlike pool; no pavement blemished the setting. The years since have seen several changes to improve safety and to qualify the facilities for use in swim meets, but despite the face-lifts, the area retains much of its early charm.

The first major change to the pool was made in 1937, with the remodeling, enlarging, and modernizing of the bathhouse, originally of Spanish architecture and with an elevated porch. In 1948, the entire swimming area was renovated, with a concrete path constructed around the edge to replace the original stepping-stones and with the pool itself Gunited. A new filter, circulation, and vacuum system were also put in at that time. After the strengthening of the Lake Cascade dam in 1965, use of the waterfall was discontinued. Twenty-five-yard lanes and an island added in 1966 qualify the facilities for swim competitions. To cut the costs of insurance, the diving board was removed in 1987 and the area fenced.

71

Teen-aged girls perform a September Aquacade in front of the renovated bathhouse in the 1940s. ◄

Under swim instructor Frank Russ, Orinda's swim team entered and won its first meet against Diablo and Claremont country clubs in 1935. In 1946, Gil Callies took over. He organized the Aquacades, a popular program of water ballet put on by teen-aged women over Labor Day weekend. Following Callies, Gary Kearney became swim instructor in 1959 and continued the Aquacades tradition for two more years. But Kearney also put much energy into developing a swim team, and with the growing interest in competitive swimming, the popularity of the Aquacades diminished.

The OCC swim team, Jaws, began intense competition after head coach and pool manager Bill Brown joined Orinda's staff in 1967. Brown, also water polo coach at Miramonte High School, hired staff members Kit Skow and Kathy Phillips—now Kathy Skow—to complete his staff, and the three began building a high-powered program for children, offering free lessons to the youngsters and developing top swimmers for the team. Kathy Skow, as six-and-under coach, and Brown have remained with the Club.

Jaws, with the continued support of family members, won its first All Orinda meet in 1970 and continued to win that meet for seven years straight. The team brought great pride to the Club in 1972 when its nearly ninety members won eight dual meets, the All Orinda meet, and the County Championship, thus becoming the first team to accomplish this record in one season.

Today's program includes some two dozen annual meets for team members, private and group swim lessons for everyone from newborn up, and outside social gatherings for participants about every ten days.

THE PEOPLE

Male swimmers at Orinda have also fared well. Pete Schnugg and Drew McDonald both swam on the U.S. Olympic water polo team in 1980, and McDonald also competed at the 1984 Olympics in Los Angeles, where his team won a silver medal. Kirk Everist swims with the U.S. National Junior Water Polo Team in preparation for the 1992 Olympics. All have competed worldwide.

High-school all-American swimmers from Orinda have included Liz Cunha, Kirk Everist, Ron Laher, Steve Millham, and Molly Stryker. All-American high-school water polo players have been Chris Chiappone, Kirk Everist, Kevin Lydon, Drew McDonald, Trent McDonald, Steve Millham, Pat Nelson, and John, Pete, and Tom Schnugg.

Among Orinda's early swimmers coached by Gil Callies in the late forties was a young lady named Barbara Stark who swam in the Olympics in Helsinki in 1952 and later became an instructor of women's swimming at UC Berkeley. Another Orinda member, Karen Moe, set a world record in the butterfly during the sixties, when she swam at OCC. Moe swam in the Olympics in Munich in 1972 and won a gold medal in the butterfly. Again she swam in the 1976 Olympics in Quebec, this time as Karen Moe Thornton, aged twenty-four, the oldest member of the U.S. team. There she placed fourth and set a new U.S. record in the butterfly. Moe Thornton began coaching the women's swim team at UC Berkeley in 1979.

OPPOSITE *Diving was popular at OCC until the board was removed in 1987 because of increased insurance costs.*

Bill Brown, OCC's pool manager for more than twenty years, started a tradition of intense competitiveness for the Club team, Jaws. ◄

Tennis

Although the first tennis court near the swimming pool was constructed in 1926, according to E. I.'s promise to the original Club members, it suffered long periods of neglect before the beginning of Orinda's formal tennis program in 1950. The second and third courts, near the first, were added in 1956, with two near Lake Cascade following in 1964 and another two there in 1965. The eighth court and the new tennis shop near the lake were completed in 1974, leaving the old shop near the pool as a retreat for junior tennis players. This retreat was remodeled in 1990 with a recreation room, offices, restrooms, and storage space.

Discussion regarding lights at the courts over the lake began in 1979, drawing much protest from neighbors, who pointed out that the 1974 permit to build the courts had prohibited lighting them. The county finally granted approval for the lights in 1982 so that Orinda members could enjoy evening games.

Kevin Merrick, Orinda's tennis pro, has coached three generations of OCC tennis players.

78

In 1950, with OCC's single court overgrown by rose bushes, its decks used mostly as a grandstand for golf spectators, Beatrice Martin began the push for a formal tennis program for the Club's young people. The court was cleared and fenced, Edgar and Emily Stewart contributed a net from their former home, and a program was under way.

Martin, known as Bea, felt that young people could learn etiquette, be introduced to other young people, and participate in good, wholesome outdoor activity through tennis. She located George Russell, the first coach, and found him a place to live in Orinda. Bea also sponsored a junior mixed doubles tournament, concluding with a barbecue, dinner-dance, and trophies, which she continued to support until the tennis pro took over the program.

Bea, too, was responsible for locating Orinda's current pro, Kevin Merrick, in 1957. She had heard of the young man in the East Bay "who was the best tennis pro in the Western United States" and convinced then-General Manager Clarke Mathews to persuade the Claremont

Country Club to release Merrick from his contract. Under Merrick's guidance at OCC, the tennis program exploded; by the late sixties, the Club was running about twenty events per year.

Among Orinda's most popular tennis programs has been its Easter Vacation Orinda Junior Tennis Tournament, beginning in 1958. Hundreds of youngsters, including state and national stars, came to the Bay Area each spring to compete—despite the fact that it always rained. The yearly event demanded much planning and scheduling of outside courts, transportation, meals, and accommodations for participants. At times, the tournament would use up to twenty-six outside courts, in addition to those at OCC.

Since 1987, the father-son tournament around Easter time has been popular. The summer tennis camp is another highlight for children, begun when Jeff Southwick came as assistant pro. The OCC Grand Prix, instituted in 1984, gives youngsters a chance to earn trophies based on participation.

Senior tournaments were initiated in the 1960s. The earlier tournaments were open to players from thirty-five years of age up; in the more recent tournaments, competitors sixty years and up compete, with the newest category, added in 1991, for those over eighty.

In 1976, a group of male members calling themselves the Bluebirds began meeting casually on Saturday mornings for play. These pickup games have remained popular for men.

Merrick led the first tennis players' trip abroad when the group traveled to the Wimbledon Centennial in 1978. He also led five groups to Mexico during the 1980s.

Orinda became a part of the Orinda Adult Tennis League with teams from Sleepy Hollow, Orinda Woods, and the Moraga Tennis Club in 1977.

Early tennis players enjoyed use of the first court built in 1926, one of Orinda's initial attractions.

Orinda's adult tennis shop was built lakeside in 1974.

Orinda's junior tennis team brought the Club special pride with the Northern California Junior Davis Cup Championship in 1979.

Orinda has hosted such guest tennis stars as Billie Jean King, who played here in an exhibition match with OCC member Lynne Abbes in 1966. The following year, Abbes went to Wimbledon. She had placed first at Orinda as a nine-year-old in 1959 and had entered national competition at age eleven. Currently Abbes works as a pro for the U.S. Tennis Association. Other OCC players now employed as tennis pros are Ren Kern, Ron Noon, and Brad Rieser.

The Orindan

The first *Orindan*, published in 1927, was more than a Club newsletter; it was a news sheet for the entire Orinda community. Editor Warren Harold was a member of OCC and a real estate agent in Orinda. Most Orinda families at the time were also OCC members. The newsletter continued until 1952, when it was discontinued. Starting monthly publication again in 1961, Editor Bobbie McGuire wrote, "THE ORINDAN will be published to stimulate interest and participation in your Club . . . if this doesn't do it . . . better stick with martinis and gimlets!"

For four consecutive years, beginning in 1989, *The Orindan* has placed first in the private club division of the NCGA's contest for club publications. Entries are judged on appearance, contents, and service to members.

Social Events

Through the years, OCC has offered many activities for its members, some annually for many years, others only once or a few times. Among those lasting for long periods of time have been the Fourth of July celebration, with a tournament, dinner-dance, and fireworks over Lake Cascade in the early years; the summer barbecue and squire dances; the Christmas buffets; the New Year's Eve extravaganzas; the father-daughter dances; the father-son sports-dinners; and St. Patrick's Day welcome dances for new members. Many theme parties, crab feeds, and bus trips to Stanford for the Big Game against UC Berkeley—or dinner-dances at the Club when the football game is in Berkeley—have also filled the calendars.

86

One short-lived event that all those attending still remember with great fondness was *The Foolies* of 1963 through 1966. Members rehearsed weeks in advance to perform songs, dances, and skits for this vaudevillian spoof of life in Orinda. Others worked to create elaborate costumes or to help behind the scenes. At the performances, packed audiences roared with laughter and applause. When it was all over, cast celebrations continued into the early hours.

OPPOSITE *Performers meet applause during the grand finale of a 1960s Foolies.*

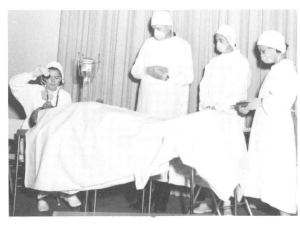

WHEN I WAS A LAD . . .

To the music of "When I Was a Lad" from Gilbert & Sullivan's HMS Pinafore

When I was a lad I served a spell
As caddy on the golf course, and I did
    quite well.
I looked for balls both high and low,
And I polished all the golf clubs for the
    golfing pro.

CHORUS: And he polished all the golf
    clubs for the golfing pro.

I polished those clubs so well, you see,
That now I am the president of OCC.

CHORUS: He polished those clubs so
    well, you see,
That now he is the president of OCC.

I displayed such great proficiency
That I was asked to join the great society.
I bowed to each member with such
    charm and grace,
And always had a stupid grin
    upon my face.

CHORUS: And always had a stupid grin
    upon his face.

I worked at this role so diligently
That now I am the president of OCC.

CHORUS: He worked at this role so
    diligently
That now he is the president of OCC.

As a member I took every opportunity
To sign every chit with overt joy and glee.
I signed my name with ink and quill,
And every month the club would always
    send a bill.

CHORUS: And every month the club
    would always send a bill.

I paid my bill so delinquently
That now I am the president of OCC.

CHORUS: He paid his bill so
    delinquently
That now he is the president of OCC.

If you want my advice, be guided by
    this rule:
Don't ever volunteer; don't be a
    great big fool.
Don't raise your hand to accept a
    club job,
Don't smile at anyone; just be a
    first-class snob.

CHORUS: Don't smile at anyone; just be
    a first-class snob.
Stick close to your desk, and you will
    never be,

ENTIRE GROUP: Never be the president
    of OCC.

Lyrics written and sung by
Earle Cunha, OCC President,
during the 1965 Foolies

89

90

In 1974, the Club celebrated its fiftieth anniversary with great fanfare. Throughout one weekend in June, the event featured golf and tennis tournaments, pool activities, a "Cavalcade of Nostalgia" (with historic vehicles, fashion shows, and movie star impersonations), a barbecue, an old-timers' dinner, a fashion show of styles from the twenties, a hot-air balloon, and tug-of-war contests for all, with members signing in advance to participate and a jitney service from the Orinda BART station.

The official celebration lasted from June 4, 1974, with the first round of the ladies' Golden Bee Tournament, to June 16, 1975, with a Sunday picnic social: The entire year was packed with celebration. At the Easter egg hunt, fifty golden eggs were hidden; tennis members competed in a contest called "Around the Club through Fifty Years"; and the Club tour, to Spain and England, was designated as an anniversary trip.

Looking Ahead

With a current membership of some 840, Orinda Country Club is now a member of the National Club Association and the California State Club Association. Still it evolves to meet the requests and needs of the membership. Golf-course changes will be required by the vast increase in the number of rounds played; the clubhouse decor will be altered again and again; and new plantings will probably replace older choices. New tournaments will be established and old ones discontinued. New committees will be formed as needs and interests change: The Community Relations Committee, established in 1988, and the Wine Committee, to select vintages for the dining room in the 1980s, are only two of the many that have already joined the original four set up by the first board of directors.

What will not change is the Club's spirit: the congeniality, the companionship of family and friends, the serenity of playing in the sunshine on Orinda's scenic hills.

E. I. deLaveaga loved his land. For thousands of OCC members past and present, it is a great legacy that he was able to see his dream of sharing a vision come true.

THE PRESIDENTS

Orinda Country Club Presidents
(with first year of election)

Jimmy L'Hommedieu, 1924
Herbert C. Capwell, 1925
Arthur V. Sherry, 1928
Peter F. Scott, 1932
Frank D. Bryant, 1934
A. G. Strong, 1936
Walter Henderson, 1940
E. L. Jeff Hedemark, 1942
Francis Pelletier, 1946
James E. DeArmond, 1948
George Lauer, 1949
Lloyd O'Connell, 1952
John McDonnell, 1954
Donald Phipps, 1955
Walter Boysen, 1956
William McNevin, 1957

Donald E. Doten, 1958
Robert B. Johnson, 1961
Ramsay Underwood, 1963
William J. McGuire, 1964
Earle Cunha, 1965
Francis A. Watson, Jr., 1967
Robert J. Foley, 1968
A. V. Scollard, 1970
John C. Loper, 1972
Howard W. Crandall, 1974
Edwin A. Flinn, Jr. , 1976
Homer T. Anderson, 1977
B. Frank Brunk, Jr., 1978
Richard H. Gorman, 1979
Russell T. Bigelow, 1980
David A. Woolsey, 1981
William L. Gonser, 1982
George P. Vila, 1983
Neil F. Thrams, 1984
Kenneth P. Handy, 1985
Scott S. Bird, 1986
Vern P. Schafer, 1987
Austin R. Gibbons, 1988
David R. Tripaldi, 1989
John Sears, 1990
Douglas C. Gillespie, 1991
Robert J. Sciutto, 1992

NORTHERN CALIFORNIA GOLF ASSOCIATION PRESIDENTS FROM ORINDA

Walter Henderson, 1943–1944

Edward R. Foley, 1955–1956

Francis A. Watson, Sr.,* 1959–1960

Donald E. Doten, 1968

Robert J. Foley, 1975

Francis A. Watson, Jr., 1983

Joseph Zablocki,** 1984

B. Frank Brunk, Jr., 1991

* Francis A. Watson, Sr., was also a member of the Mira Vista Country Club, Berkeley, and chose to represent that club when President of NCGA.

** Joseph Zablocki was a member of the Olympic Club, San Francisco, when he served.

INSIDE BACK COVER A hole-in-one at the eighth hole helped Lawson Little, Jr., to win the 1928 NCGA tournament at Orinda and launched his career as one of the country's top golfers.